SUPPORTING YOU THROUGH EVERY STAGE

STAGE 2
WORKBOOK

A study and revision aid for the BHS Stage 2 assessment

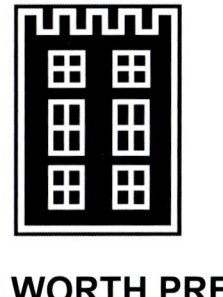

KENILWORTH PRESS

First published in the UK in 2008 by Kenilworth Press
an imprint of Quiller Publishing Ltd

Reprinted 2012, 2015, 2025

This new edition published 2018

© The British Horse Society 2008

All rights reserved. No part of this publication may be reproduced, stored in a retrieval system, or transmitted in any form or by any means, electronic, mechanical, photocopying, recording or otherwise, without the written permission of the copyright holder.

British Library Cataloguing in Publication Data
A catalogue record for this book is available from the British Library

ISBN 978 1 910016 33 6

Layout and illustrations by Carole Vincer
Revised by Arabella Ainslie
Jacket cover by Howard Taylor

Printed in UK by Short Run Press Ltd, Exeter

Appointed GPSR EU Representative:
Easy Access System Europe Oü, 16879218
Address: Mustamäe tee 50, 10621, Tallinn, Estonia
Contact Details: gpsr.requests@easproject.com, +358 40 500 3575

KENILWORTH PRESS
An imprint of Quiller Publishing Ltd
The Hill, Merrywalks, Stroud
Gloucestershire, GL5 4EP
Tel: 01453 847800
Email: info@quillerbooks.com
Website: www.quillerpublishing.com

DISCLAIMER: The authors and publishers shall have neither liability nor responsibility to any person or entity with respect to any loss or damage caused or alleged to be caused directly or indirectly by the information contained in this book. While the book is as accurate as the authors can make it, there may be errors, omissions, and inaccuracies.

CONTENTS

Introduction | 4

QUESTIONS
1 Plaiting | 5
2 Bandages and Travel Equipment | 6
3 Saddlery | 10
4 Handling and Lungeing | 15
5 Stable Design | 20
6 Shoeing | 23
7 Trimming | 25
8 Anatomy and Physiology | 26
9 Horse Behaviour | 30
10 Horse Health | 33
11 Fittening | 39
12 Grassland Care | 42
13 Feeding | 45
14 Riding | 48

ANSWERS | 54

Further Reading | 77
Useful Addresses | 78

INTRODUCTION

This workbook has been compiled as a revision aid for candidates preparing for the BHS Stage 2 care, ride and lunge assessments. It is designed to be used in conjunction with a Stage 2 course, ideally provided by a BHS Approved Training Centre, where coaches have a good understanding of the BHS Equine Excellence Pathway.

The questions have been written to captivate the imagination and help to make revision and quizzing of knowledge entertaining, whilst maintaining the integrity and quality of the assessment for which the student is preparing.

The authors wish to stress that there is no 'BHS way' for either practical or theory. As such there may be more answers to questions than have been given. The BHS system aims to train practical, safe and efficient horsemen and women, thus providing a foundation of internationally recognised qualifications from which a person may develop in any equestrian direction.

Details of further reading and contact details for the BHS are given at the end of the book.

BHS revision workbooks are available for Stage 1 and Stage 2

1 PLAITING

Q1.1 (a) When plaiting, why do we use an odd number of plaits along the neck (making an even number when including the forelock)?
(b) If the horse has a short or long neck, can this be helped visually and, if so, how?
(c) Describe how to plait a mane correctly, as shown in the drawings A – E.

(a) _____

_____

(b) _____

_____

_____

(c) A _____

B _____

C _____

D _____

E _____

Q1.2 (a) What is the difference between a 'flat' and a 'ridge' tail plait?
(b) Compare these two tail plaits. Write down why you think one is well plaited and the other poorly plaited.

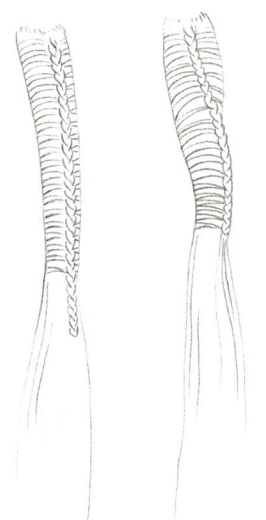

(a) _____

_____

(b) _____

_____

_____

_____

2 BANDAGES AND TRAVEL EQUIPMENT

Q2.1 Give four reasons for using stable bandages.

1. _____
2. _____
3. _____
4. _____

Q2.2 The following pictures show the correct procedure for applying a stable bandage. Describe each picture.

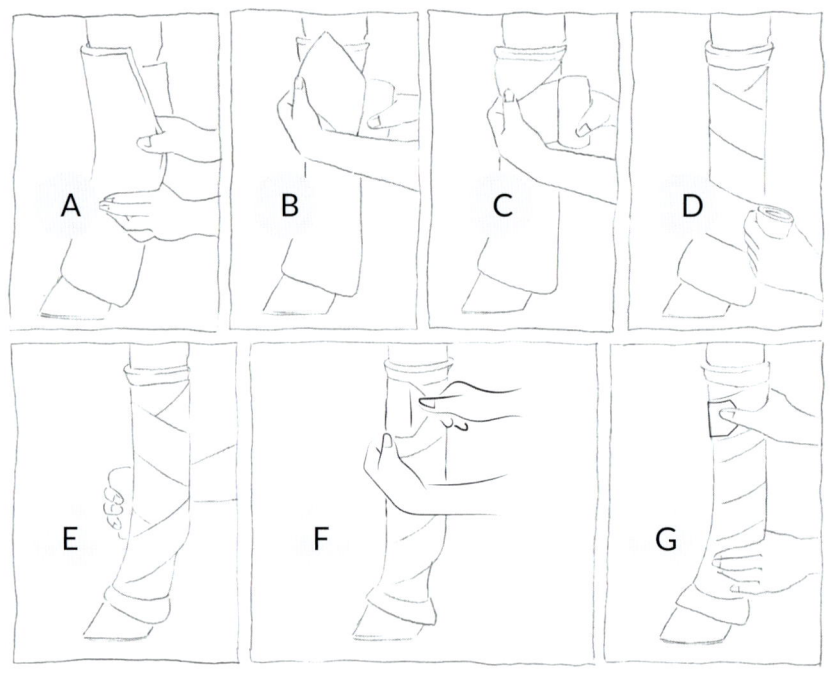

A _____

B _____

C _____

D _____

E _____

F _____

G _____

6

Q2.3 Below is a sequence of images for putting on a tail bandage, but the order is jumbled. Match the sentences to the drawings to describe the correct sequence.

5 return back up the tail   6 tie tapes on the side
4 wrap evenly all the way down to the base of the tail   1 start the bandage with the end flap out
7 fold the last wrap over the bow   3 roll bandage over flap   2 fold flap over

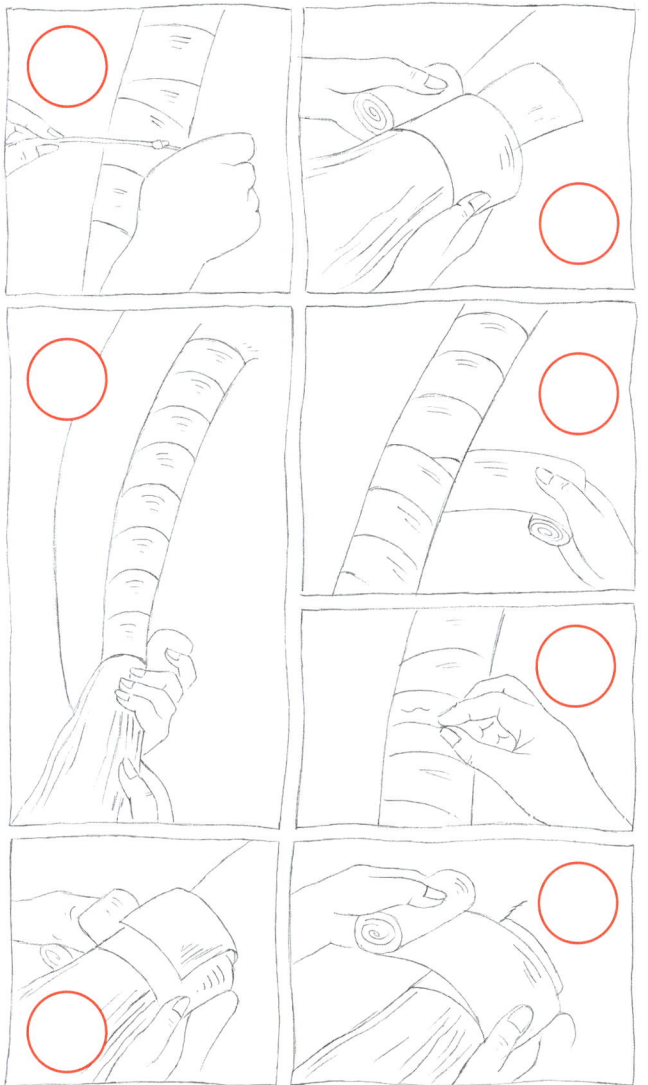

Q2.4 Fill in the missing words to describe how you would remove a tail bandage.

bandage   untie   slide

To remove a tail bandage, firstly _____ the tapes and possibly loosen the first few wraps of the

_____. Holding the top of the bandage, gently _____ it down the tail. Re-roll ready for use.

2 BANDAGES AND TRAVEL EQUIPMENT

Q2.5 What is the difference between Fybagee for stable bandages and Fybagee for travelling bandages?

___

Q2.6 What are the consequences of poor bandaging?

___

Q2.7 List the equipment used for travelling and state the purpose of each item.

___

2 BANDAGES AND TRAVEL EQUIPMENT

Q2.8 Fill in the gaps to explain how to apply and fit travel boots.

> correctly   slippage   centre   strap   clean

Tie the horse up securely. On _____, dry legs fit each boot individually, positioning _____ and then fastening. When fastening, start with the middle _____ and work up and down the leg from the _____ out. Fasten firmly into position, ensuring no _____.

Q2.9 What are the dangers of using travelling boots/bandages that are not correctly fitted?

_____

_____

_____

_____

Q2.10 Describe how you would clean and store the following?

RUGS

_____

BOOTS

_____

BANDAGES

_____

FYBAGEE

_____

ALL

_____

3 SADDLERY

Q3.1 Looking at the image of this well-fitting saddle below, list the points to check when fitting a saddle.

SIZE	
LEVEL	
POMMEL CLEARANCE	
GULLET	
SHOULDER	
BEARING SURFACE	

Q3.2 Look at these drawings and decide which would be suitable for:
(a) dressage   (b) show jumping   (c) cross-country

3 SADDLERY

Q3.3 List five possible consequences for horse or rider if ill-fitting tack is used.

1. _____
2. _____
3. _____
4. _____
5. _____

Q3.4 Look at this horse tacked up for lungeing. Give an explanation of the fit of each item of equipment.

BRIDLE	
CAVESSON	
SADDLE	
SIDE REINS	
BOOTS	
LUNGE LINE	

3 SADDLERY

Q3.5 List the points to check for comfort on each part of the bridle.

BIT	
BROWBAND	
NOSEBAND	
THROATLASH	
CHEEKPIECES	

Q3.6 Describe how to fit the following nosebands.

FLASH	
DROP	
GRACKLE	

3 SADDLERY

Q3.7 Identify and give the function of each boot below.

BOOT	FUNCTION

13

3 SADDLERY

Q3.8 What would you look for when checking the fit of a hunting breastplate whilst tacking up?

_____
_____
_____
_____

Q3.9 Explain the purpose of each stage of tack cleaning.

WARM WATER	
OIL	
SADDLE SOAP	

Q3.10 Imagine that there are pieces of tack that need to be stored. Explain your preparation of the tack and how you would store it.

_____
_____
_____
_____

4 HANDLING AND LUNGEING

Q4.1 Fill in this risk assessment for different aspects of yard work and state what preventative measures you would take for each risk.

RISK	MUCKING OUT	TACKING UP	LEADING
SELF			
HORSE			
OTHERS			

Q4.2 Circle the qualities that you feel would help a groom to maintain the confidence and control of horses.

Patient

Intolerant

Quiet

Quick tempered

Assertive

Efficient

Organised

Relaxed

4 HANDLING AND LUNGEING

Q4.3 How do you prepare the vehicle for loading?

Q4.4 Describe how to load a horse into a lorry or trailer.

Q4.5 Describe how to unload a horse.

4 HANDLING AND LUNGEING

Q4.6 List five reasons for lungeing.

1. _____
2. _____
3. _____
4. _____
5. _____

Q4.7 The two people lungeing below show very different stances. One will appear confident to the horse, the other, not. List the differences in body language.

A   B

A
_____
_____
_____
_____
_____
_____

B
_____
_____
_____
_____
_____
_____

4 HANDLING AND LUNGEING

Q4.8 What 'feel' should you have at the end of the lunge line?

_____

_____

Q4.9 List two main rules to follow when you are lungeing.

_____

_____

Q4.10 Explain the benefits of each of these when lungeing.

WALK	
TROT	
CIRCLE	
TRANSITIONS	
CANTER	

4 HANDLING AND LUNGEING

Q4.11 Give the reasons for using each part of the lungeing equipment.

CAVESSON	

SIDE REINS	

BRUSHING BOOTS	

LUNGE LINE	

SADDLE/ROLLER	

LUNGE WHIP	

Q4.12 Why must the handler wear a hat, gloves and correct footwear when lungeing?

_____

_____

_____

5 STABLE DESIGN

Q5.1 List one advantage and disadvantage of each of the stable materials below.

	ADVANTAGE	DISADVANTAGE
WALLS		
Breeze block		
Brick		
Wood		
ROOF		
Tiles		
Plywood and felt		
Onduline		
FLOOR		
Brick		
Concrete		
Rubber Matting		

Q5.2 Complete the table of ideal stable dimensions.

	16hh HORSE	PONY
SIZE		
HEIGHT		
DOOR WIDTH		
DOOR HEIGHT		
HALF DOOR HEIGHT		

Q5.3 (a) List three methods of ventilating stables.
(b) Why is ventilation in stables important?

(a) _____

_____

_____

(b) _____

_____

5 STABLE DESIGN

Q5.4 (a) Why is good drainage necessary in stabling, and in which direction should the floor slope?
(b) What are the possible results of poor drainage?

(a) _____

(b) _____

_____

_____

_____

_____

Q5.5 Complete the table to include essential and extra stable fittings.

ESSENTIAL	EXTRA

Q5.6 Why should there be as few stable fittings as possible?

6 SHOEING

Q6.1 Identify these farrier's tools and explain the purpose of each.

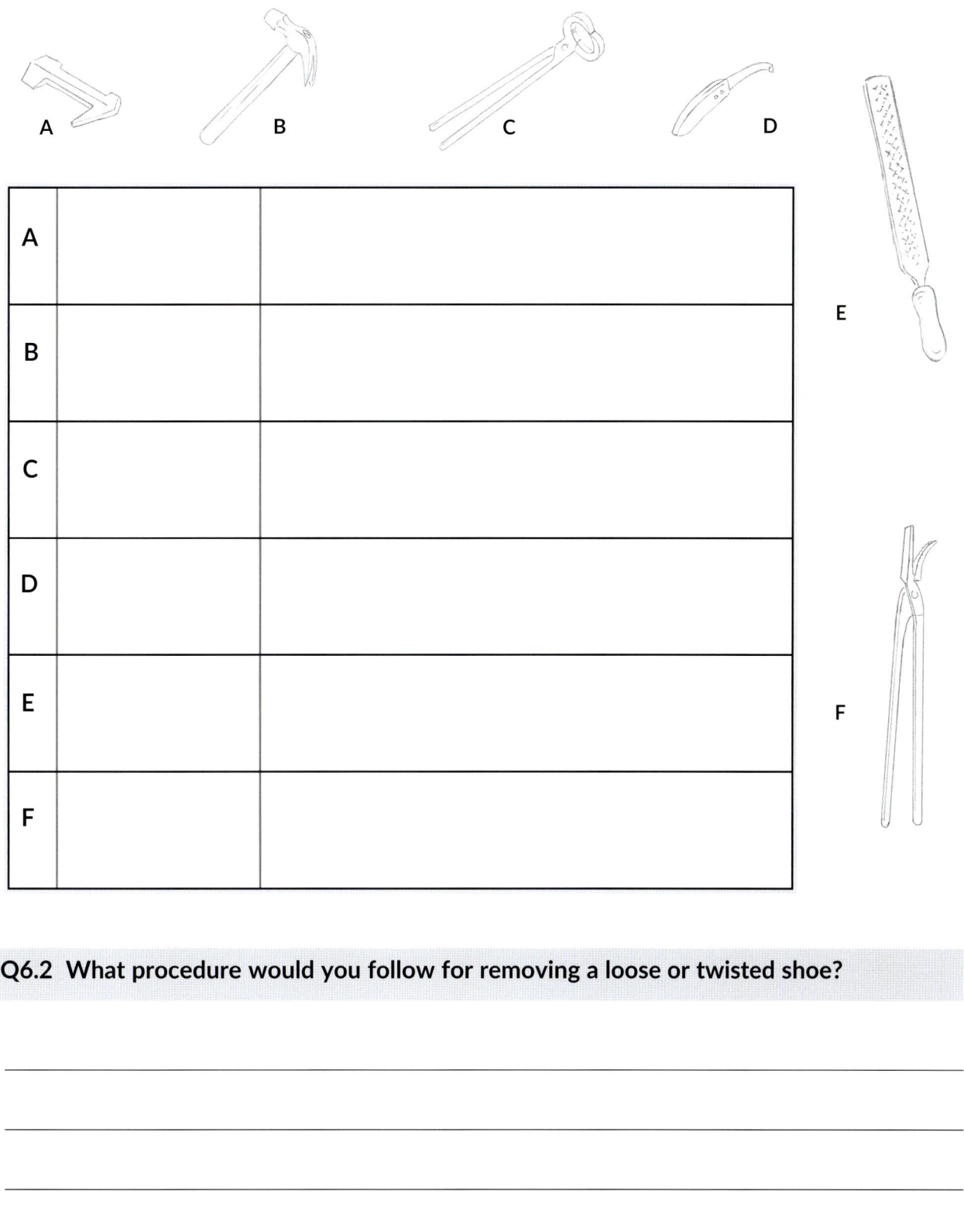

A		
B		
C		
D		
E		
F		

Q6.2 What procedure would you follow for removing a loose or twisted shoe?

___
___
___
___

6 SHOEING

Q6.3 The pictures below show possible problems that can arise from infrequent shoeing. Identify each.

Q6.4 Explain the possible consequences of each of the problems in Q6.3.

Q6.5 Looking at the pictures, what problems may occur if unshod hooves are not trimmed regularly?

7 TRIMMING

Q7.1 Looking at the horse below, label the areas that can be trimmed.

Q7.2 Describe how to trim three of the areas you have labelled.

_____

_____

_____

Q7.3 List two reasons why you would not trim a horse.

_____

_____

Q7.4 Circle the correct reasons for pulling a mane.

- Shows off the horse's neck
- Makes the mane lie better
- Thins the mane
- Makes the mane thicker
- Easier to plait
- Makes the mane longer
- Makes the mane less greasy

8 ANATOMY AND PHYSIOLOGY

Q8.1 On the diagram below, label the horse's internal organs.

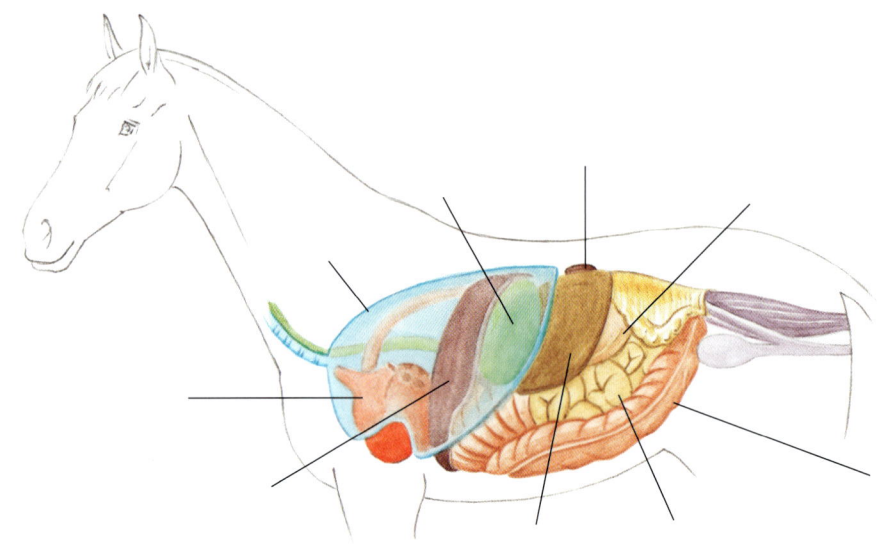

Q8.2 On this diagram of the digestive system, from mouth to small intestine, label each part, and then briefly describe its function.

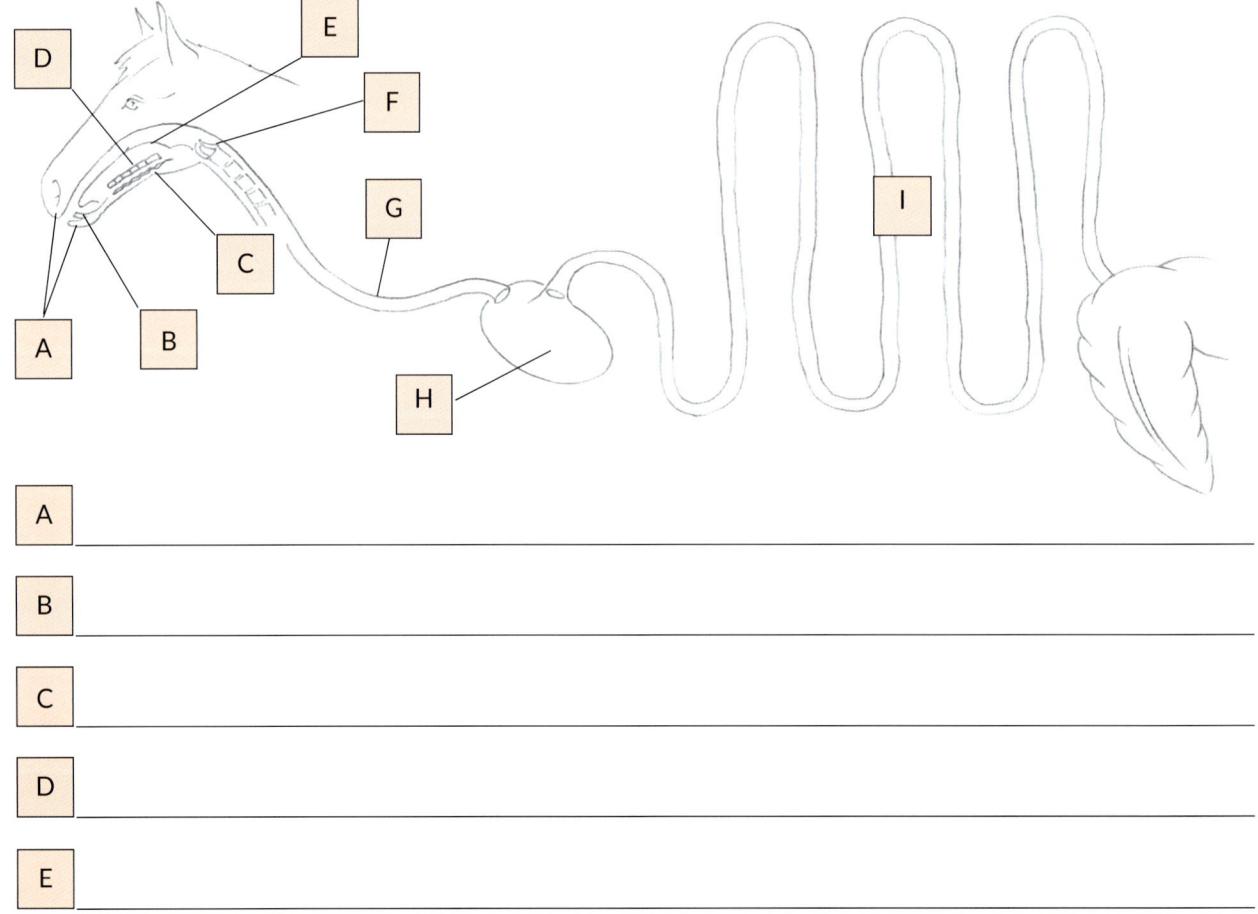

A _____

B _____

C _____

D _____

E _____

F _____

G _____

H _____

I _____

_____

_____

_____

Q8.3 Here is a diagram of the second half of the digestive system. Label each part, and then briefly describe its function.

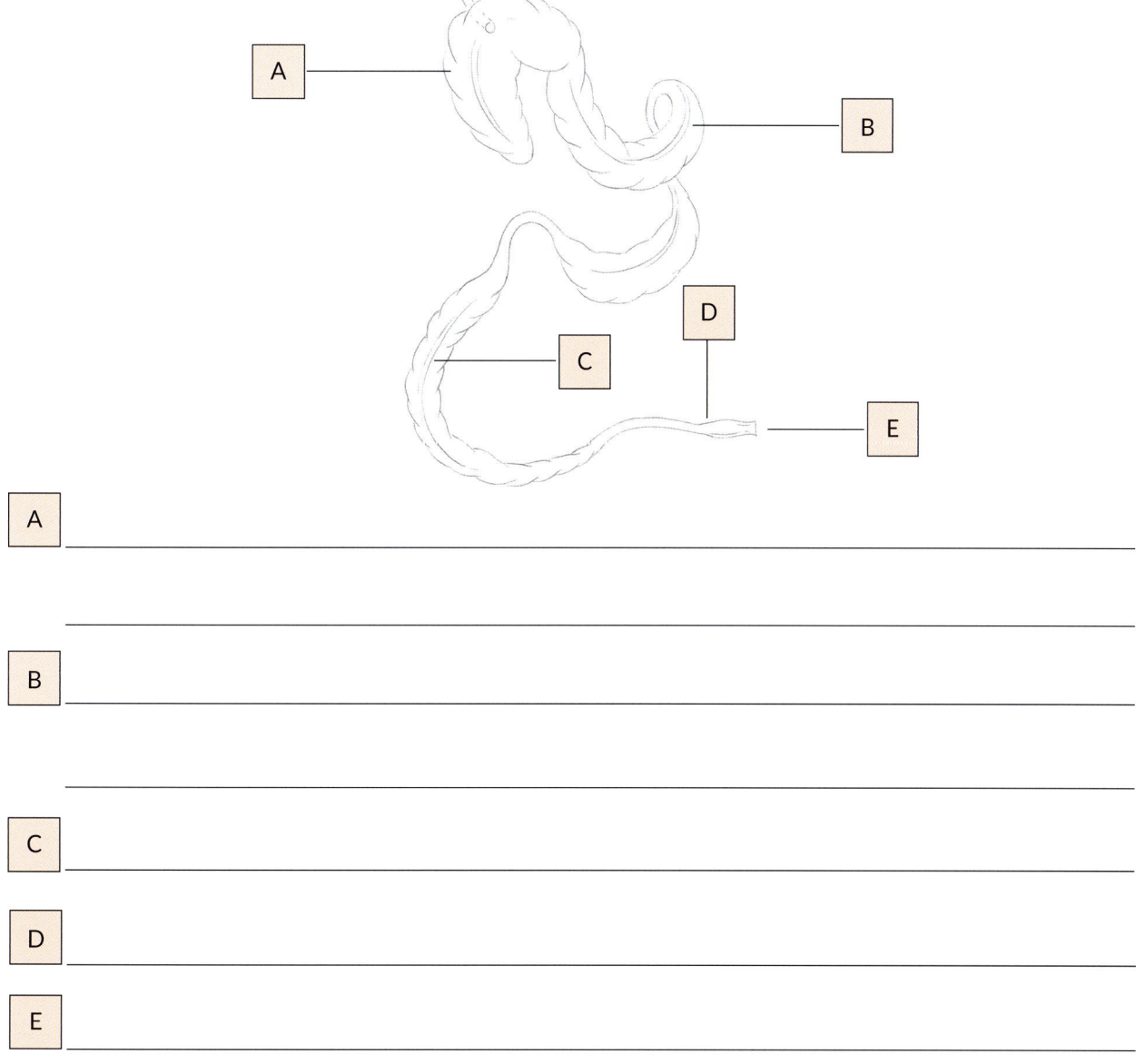

A _____

B _____

C _____

D _____

E _____

27

8 ANATOMY AND PHYSIOLOGY

Q8.4 Why is forage important to the horse's digestive system?

_____

_____

Q8.5 Label the bones in the horse's skeleton.

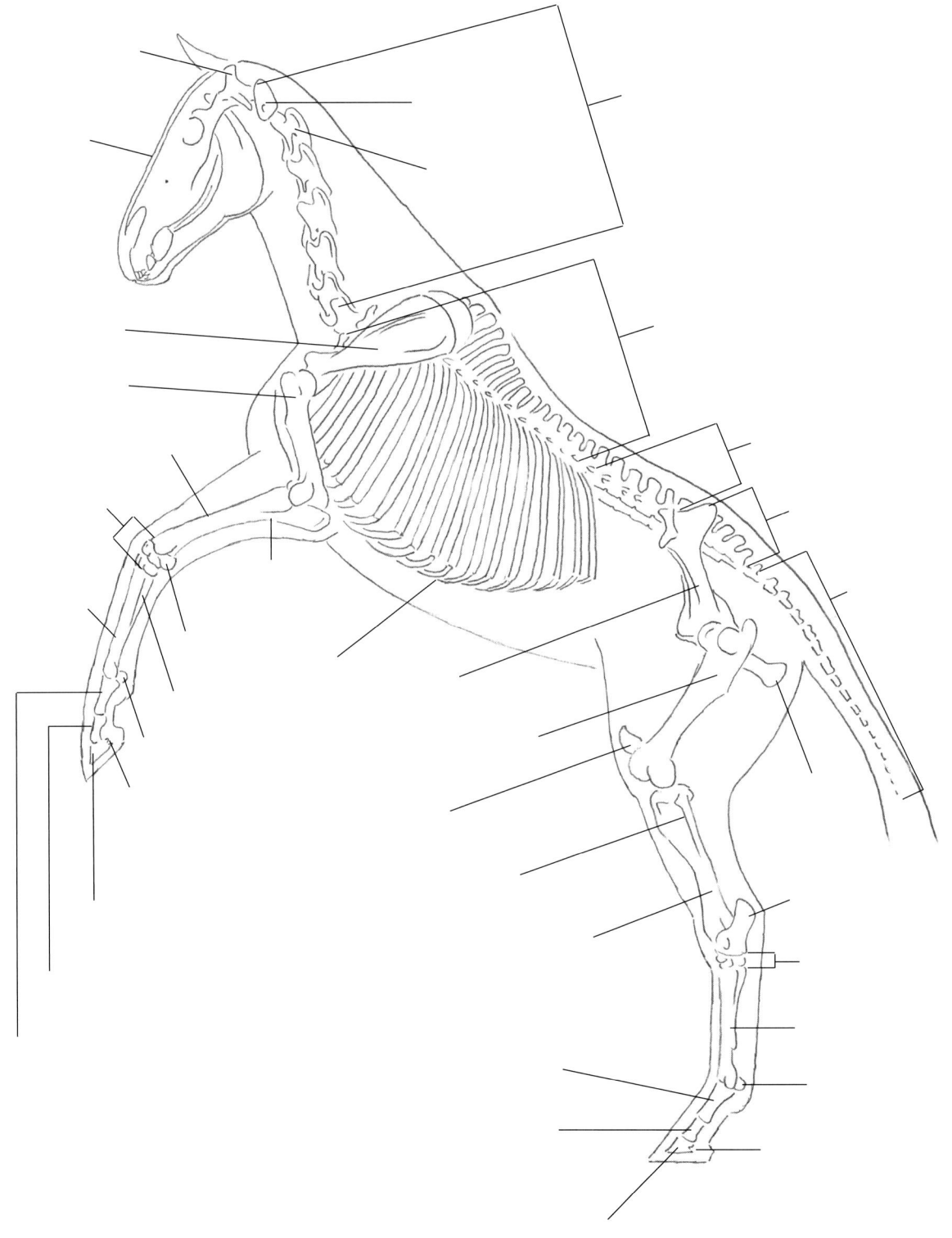

8 ANATOMY AND PHYSIOLOGY

Q8.6 Identify the external parts of the horse's foot, and briefly give a description of the role/function of parts A, C, D, G, H, I and K.

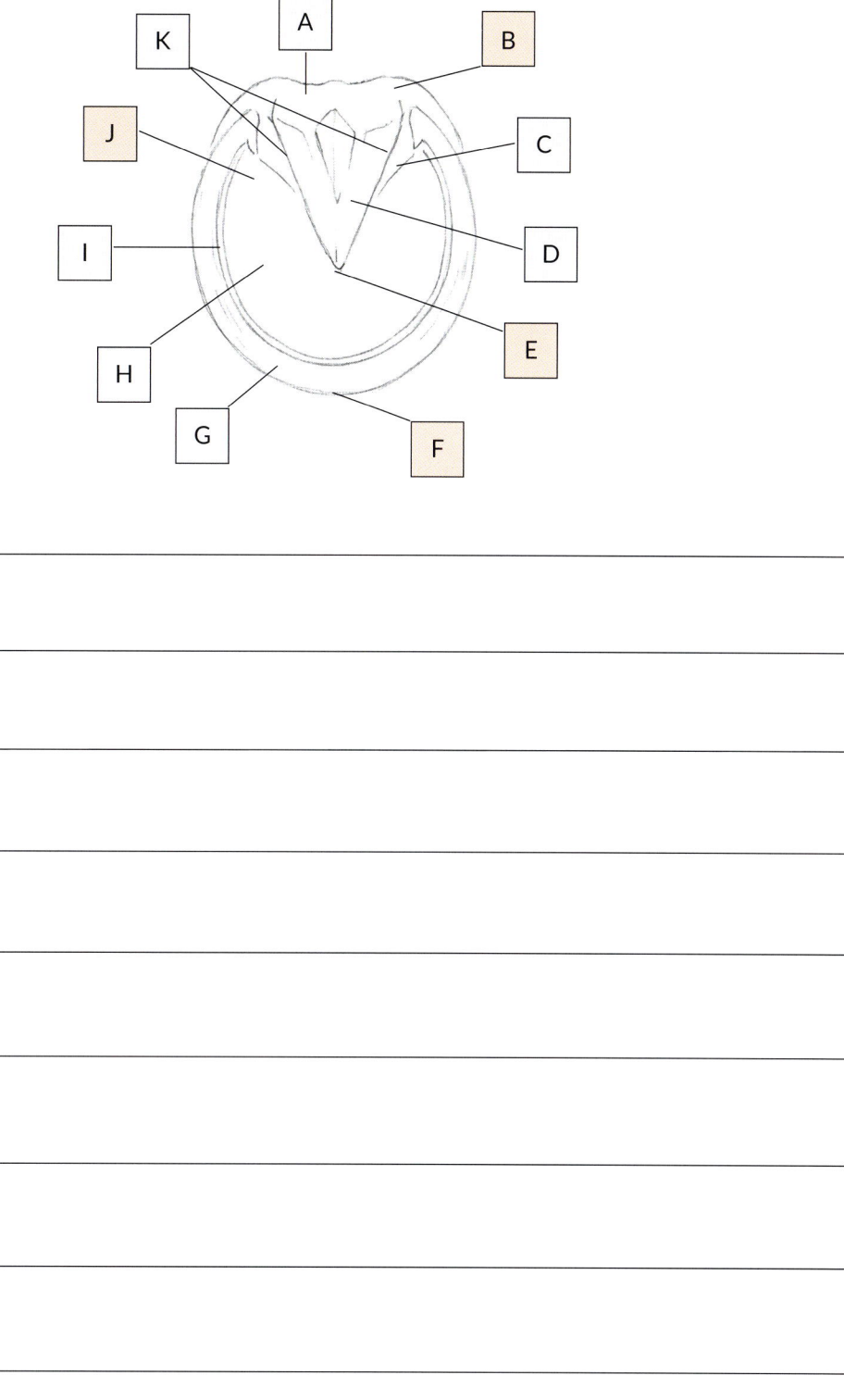

A _____

B _____

C _____

D _____

E _____

F _____

G _____

H _____

I _____

J _____

K _____

9 HORSE BEHAVIOUR

> **Q9.1** Imagine looking at a group of horses in the field. It is summer. They seem unsettled. What possible reasons could explain this behaviour?

_____

_____

_____

> **Q9.2** Look at the two images below: one shows a herd enjoying a natural lifestyle, the other shows a horse in a stable. Considering its natural lifestyle, in what ways have we changed how the domesticated horse lives?

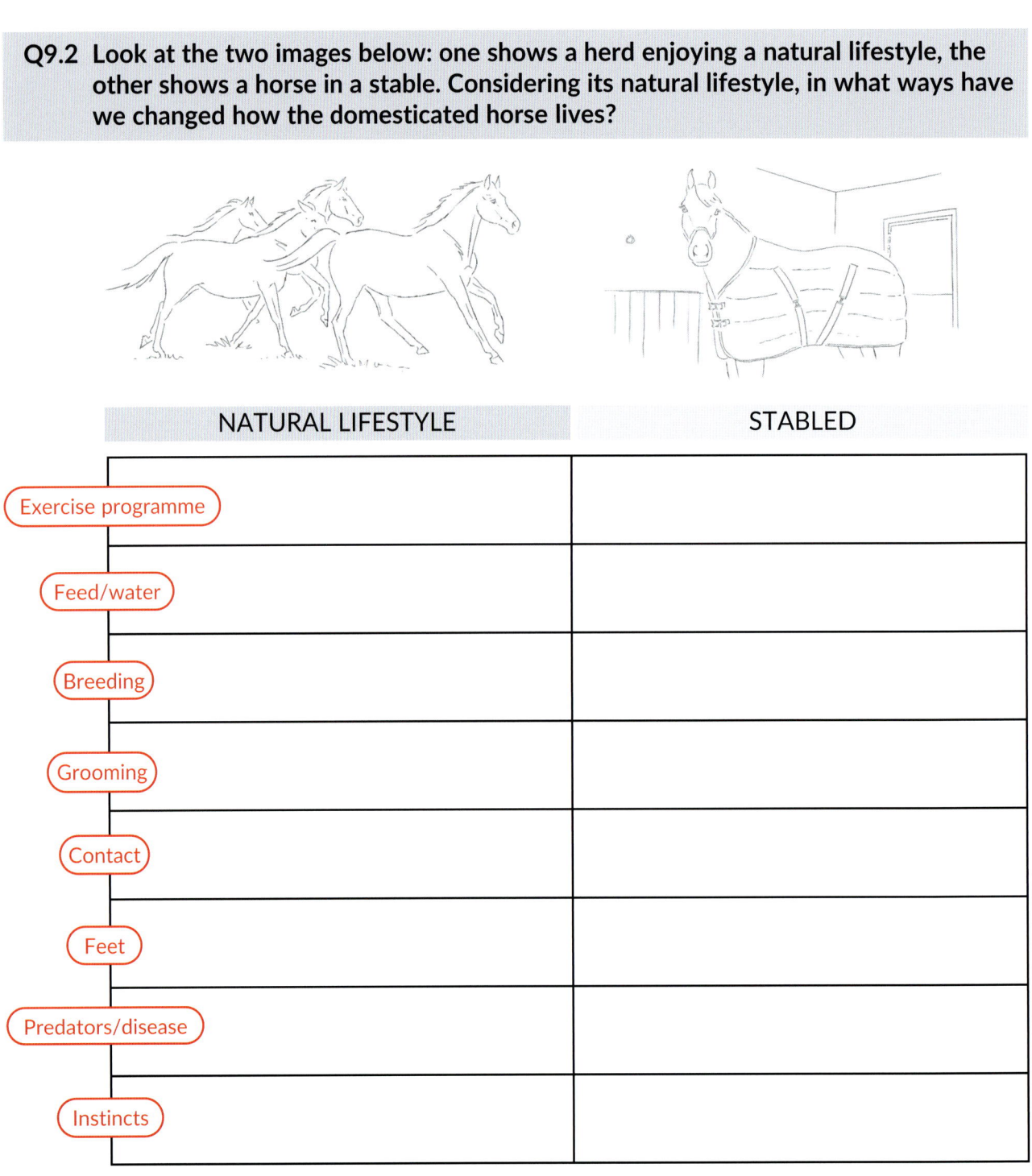

	NATURAL LIFESTYLE	STABLED
Exercise programme		
Feed/water		
Breeding		
Grooming		
Contact		
Feet		
Predators/disease		
Instincts		

Q9.3 Write down the ways in which a horse may indicate that he is nervous in the various situations below.

Stable

Field

Ridden in the school

Ridden on the road

Jumping

Being led

Q9.4 Why might a stabled horse be difficult to catch when turned out?

___
___
___
___
___
___

9 HORSE BEHAVIOUR

Q9.5 Describe the following stereotypical behaviours.

a) Crib-biting _____

b) Box-walking _____

c) Weaving _____

_____

Q9.6 List five reasons why a horse may exhibit anti-social behaviour when ridden.

Q9.7 This horse is exhibiting signs that could suggest his tack does not fit or that he is not comfortable. List the tell-tale signs shown and any others you can think of.

10 HORSE HEALTH

Q10.1 Circle the principles below which, when combined, will help to maintain horse health.

- Exercise correctly
- Underfeed the horse — he should look lean
- Follow a worming programme
- Clip appropriately
- Work the horse on hard ground daily for 1 hour to strengthen the horse's legs
- Rug appropriately
- Routine checks — dentist, chiropractor
- Work the horse in deep going to strengthen the tendons
- Regular attention to the horse's feet
- Follow the rules of feeding

Q10.2 List the horse's normal temperature, pulse and respiration rates and explain how the following indicate signs of good/poor health.

TEMPERATURE		
PULSE		
RESPIRATION		

Q10.3 Explain how the following indicate signs of good/poor health.

BREATHING	
EATING	
DRINKING	
DROPPINGS	
STANCE	

10 HORSE HEALTH

Q10.4 List some signs of colic.

Q10.5 What can you do to reduce the risk of colic?

Q10.6 Describe the following types of wound.

PUNCTURE WOUND	
OPEN WOUND	
GRAZE	
BRUISE	

Q10.7 Describe how to carry out the following procedures.

CLEANING A CUT	
COLD HOSING	
TUBBING	
POULTICING A FOOT	

Q10.8 (a) What should you put on a medium lacerated wound while waiting for the vet to arrive?
(b) Which vaccination should you check is up to date?

(a) _____

_____

_____

(b) _____

10 HORSE HEALTH

Q10.9 Look at the picture below and describe how to care for a horse on box rest.

_____

_____

_____

_____

_____

_____

_____

_____

Q10.10 Looking at the list of injuries, indicate whether you would call the vet, provide basic treatment or monitor to see how the condition develops.

FIRST SIGNS OF COLIC	
MINOR LAMENESS	
HORSE SEEN QUIDDING	
SEVERE LAMENESS	
MINOR GRAZE TO THE QUARTERS	
SUSPECTED BROKEN LEGS	
HORSE A LITTLE DULL	
SERIOUS ARTERIAL BLEED	

Q10.11 What horse records do you consider essential?

Q10.12 Describe how to give a wormer to a horse.

Q10.13 List some methods of worm control for horses.

10 HORSE HEALTH

Q10.14 What signs might lead you to suspect that a horse's teeth require attention?

Q10.15 What does the equine dental technician/vet do when he/she rasps the teeth and why?

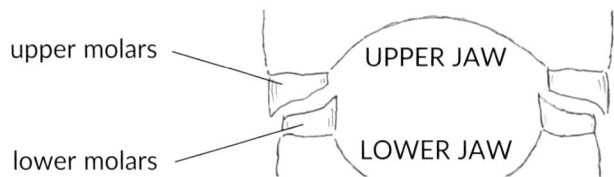

11 FITTENING

Q11.1 List some signs that would tell you a horse is not fit enough to cope with the work it is doing.

_____

Q11.2 List some reasons for using each of the following as part of a fitness programme.

HACKING	
SCHOOLING	
JUMPING/ POLE WORK	
LUNGEING	

11 FITTENING

Q11.3 What factors may influence how a horse is exercised?

_____

_____

_____

_____

Q11.4 Give four possible reasons why a horse might get coughs/colds when being brought up from grass.

1. _____

2. _____

3. _____

4. _____

Q11.5 What are the possible reasons why horses suffer from saddle sores/girth galls when beginning fittening work?

_____

_____

_____

Q11.6 Circle the conditions that could possibly cause concussion injuries and draw a rectangle around those that could cause sprain/strain injuries.

- Trotting downhill
- Fast work in deep going
- Deep going
- Jumping on a soft surface
- Hard ground
- Jumping on a hard surface
- Fast work on hard ground
- Road work in trot

Q11.7 How should a horse be cooled down after routine work?

_____
_____
_____
_____
_____

Q11.8 How should a horse be cared for after his work?

_____
_____
_____
_____
_____

12 GRASSLAND CARE

Q12.1 Below is an image of an ideal field. What could you include in your ideal field?

Q12.2 Why do hedges need cutting?

_____
_____
_____

Q12.3 List routine daily field checks.

12 GRASSLAND CARE

Q12.4 Name each of these common poisonous plants.

_____   _____   _____   _____

Q12.5 Identify these good and bad grasses and tick those that are useful in horse pasture.

_____   _____   _____

_____   _____   _____

13 FEEDING

Q13.1 Describe the following fibre feeds.

SUGAR BEET	
ALFALFA	
CHAFF	
GRASS NUTS	

Q13.2 Complete the table to describe the following cereals.

CEREAL	DESCRIPTION
Barley	
Oats	
Maize	
Peas/Beans	

Q13.3 (a) What are the considerations when feeding an older horse?
(b) What fibre and concentrate could be fed to an older horse and why?

(a) _____

_____

_____

_____

13 FEEDING

(b) _____

_____

_____

Q13.4 What might you feed a horse on box rest?

_____

_____

Q13.5 Give two examples of how you can estimate the weight of a horse.

1. _____

_____

2. _____

_____

Q13.6 Horses should be fed a minimum of 2% of their bodyweight as maintenance. Work out the minimum amount of forage each of these horses needs daily from their bodyweight.

Horse	Bodyweight (Kg)	1% of bodyweight (bodyweight ÷ 100 x 1)	(2% of bodyweight) Minimum amount of forage to feed (Kg)
BRODY	650	6.5	
CANDY	320	3.2	
FLYNN	280	2.8	
SUNNY	500	5.0	
EBONY	540	5.4	

13 FEEDING

Q13.7 The alternative fibres are hay, haylage and silage. State which are suitable for horses and give the different moisture content of each.

	HAY	HAYLAGE	SILAGE
SUITABLE FOR HORSES			
MOISTURE %			

Q13.8 Using the table, make a feed chart for the imaginary scenario below. Use as much or as little of the chart as required.

You have a yard of five horses: Galleon, Luca, Sigi, Dexter and Melody. All are fed three times per day, except Melody who does not have lunch.

Galleon, Luca and Sigi all have 5lbs (2.2kg) haylage am and lunch, and 10lbs (4.5kg) pm. They have 3lbs (1.3kg) of pony nuts am and lunch, and 4lbs (1.8kg) pm.

Dexter has 5lbs (2.2kg) haylage am and lunch, 8lbs (3.6kg) pm. He has three hard feeds, each one 3lbs (1.3kg) competition mix and 1lb (0.45kg) alfalfa. He has 10g of electrolyte supplement am only.

Melody is off work and in the field all day. She is on a maintenance diet of 100% haylage and grass: 4lbs (1.8kg) am, 8lbs (3.6kg) pm. To stop her banging she has two carrots when the others get fed.

	GALLEON am + lunch	GALLEON pm	LUCA am + lunch	LUCA pm	SIGI am + lunch	SIGI pm	DEXTER am + lunch	DEXTER pm	MELODY am	MELODY pm
HAYLAGE										
PONY NUTS										
COMPETITION NUTS										
ALFALFA										
SUPPLMENTS										
CARROTS										

14 RIDING

Q14.1 List occasions when you may need to ride with the reins in one hand.

_____

_____

Q14.2 The statements below have been made about the use of the whip. Write TRUE or FALSE at the end of each statement.

{ The whip is an object to inflict pain on the horse } { }

{ The whip is used only to make a horse go faster } { }

{ The whip should be used behind the leg to reinforce the leg aid } { }

{ The use of the whip should not interfere with the contact on the reins } { }

Q14.3 Circle the words you would pick to describe the qualities required to gain a horse's trust when riding.

- Routine
- Being quick tempered
- Negative reinforcement
- Honesty
- Repetition
- Consistency
- Positive reinforcement
- Patience
- Indecision

Q14.4 There are rules for riding in open order. List as many as you can.

_____   _____

_____   _____

_____   _____

48

Q14.5 List the rules for riding in the open in a group.

_____
_____
_____
_____

Q14.6 Undulation and ground conditions can influence the horse's speed and balance. Using a line, link the ground to the correct description.

DOWNHILL	Unbalanced
UPHILL	Faster, less balanced
SLIPPERY, GREASY	Slower, balanced
HEAVY, DEEP	Slower or faster, balanced
HARD	Slower, unbalanced

14 RIDING

Q14.7 The table below shows a description of each part of the Scale of Training. Match the names to the descriptions.

Straightness | Contact | Rhythm | Collection | Impulsion | Suppleness

NAME	DESCRIPTION
	The regularity of the gait
	The horse's ability to bend evenly on each side
	The feel you have down the rein
	The energy within a gait
	The horses hind legs follow the tracks of the front feet
	The horse lowers his hind quarters and takes more weight behind

Q14.8 Describe what each of the following aids is used for.

INSIDE LEG	

OUTSIDE LEG	

OUTSIDE REIN	

INSIDE REIN	

14 RIDING

Q14.9 What common issues do you need to be aware of when riding a circle?

1. _____
2. _____
3. _____
4. _____

Q14.10 Fill in the gaps to complete the paragraph, describing how to approach, jump and depart from a fence.

> balance   contact   jumping   canter   rhythmical   centre   quality   look up
> away   canter   corner   balance   head   jumps   secure   lead

The canter should be forward, balanced and _____. During the turn on the approach to the fence, the _____ of the canter is maintained by keeping the horse balanced between leg and hand. On the straight line approach, again the quality of the _____ is maintained. The rider guides the horse to the _____ of the fence and should _____ _____ and over the jump, focusing on the departure. As the horse _____, the rider moves forward into _____ position, allowing the horse's _____ to move forward whilst maintaining a light _____ at the end of the reins. The rider helps the horse to jump by remaining in _____ with the horse. Maintaining a _____ lower leg position allows the rider to land in _____ and immediately rebalance the horse between leg and hand, recognise the canter _____ and change it if necessary, using the next _____. The canter rhythm is re-established, if necessary, and a straight line ridden _____ from the fence, maintaining the quality of the _____ through the departure turn.

Q14.11 Why should you shorten your stirrups when preparing to jump?

_____
_____
_____

14 RIDING

Q14.12 Describe what happens in each of the following phases of the jump.

APPROACH	
TAKE OFF	
FLIGHT	
LANDING	
GETAWAY	

Q14.13 What might be the result of a rider communicating a lack of commitment or apprehension on the approach to a fence?

_____

_____

_____

_____

_____

Q14.14 What factors do you believe lead to a fluent show-jumping round?

RIDER

_____
_____
_____
_____

HORSE

_____
_____
_____
_____
_____

ANSWERS

ANSWERS

1 PLAITING

Q1.1

(a)

We use an odd number so that the eye does not visually cut the neck in half.

(b)

Long neck — fewer plaits — looks shorter.
Normal neck — 9/11/13 plaits.
Short neck — more plaits — looks longer.

(c)

A Divide the mane into equal sections.
B Plait down and secure with a band/thread.
C Fold in half.
D Fold in half again.
E Secure with a band/thread.

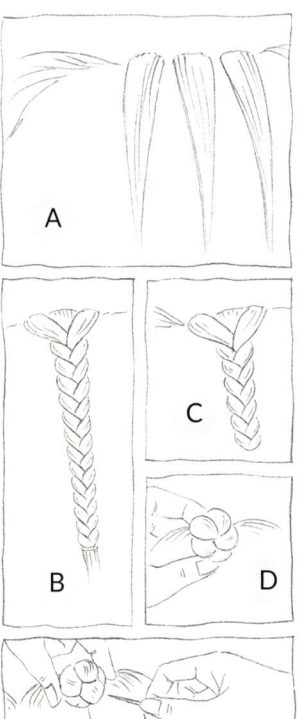

Q1.2

(a)

In a 'flat' plait the new sections are taken over and into the plait. In a 'ridge' plait the new sections are taken under and into the plait.

(b)

The first is straight, with correct-length equal sections used, tight all the way down. The second is crooked, too short, loose, and plaited using different widths of hair.

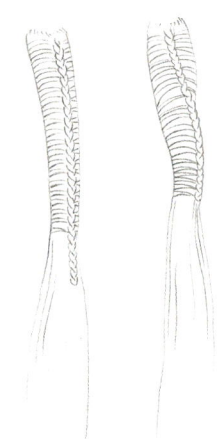

2 BANDAGES AND TRAVEL EQUIPMENT

Q2.1

Protection. Drying legs. Reducing filling. Warmth.

Q2.2

A Wrap Fybagee around the leg and fit. Overlap in the direction of bandaging, i.e. front over back.
B Begin first wrap of bandage with the end left up and out.
C Fold the protruding flap over.
D Continue to bandage, overlapping approximately half a bandage each time.
E As you reach under the fetlock, make a 'V' with the bandage at the front of the pastern.
F Fasten and finish.
G Check you can fit one finger width in the top of the bandage.

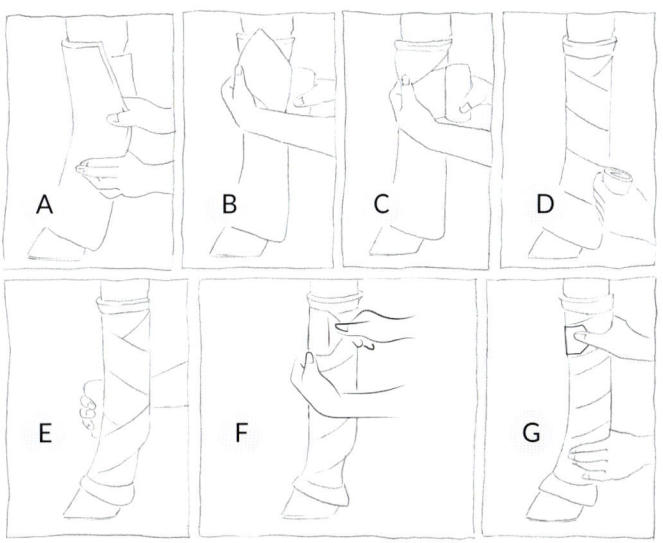

55

Q2.3

1. Start the bandage with the end flap out.
2. Fold flap over.
3. Roll bandage over flap.
4. Wrap evenly all the way down to the base of tail.
5. Return back up the tail.
6. Tie tapes on the side.
7. Fold the last wrap over the bow.

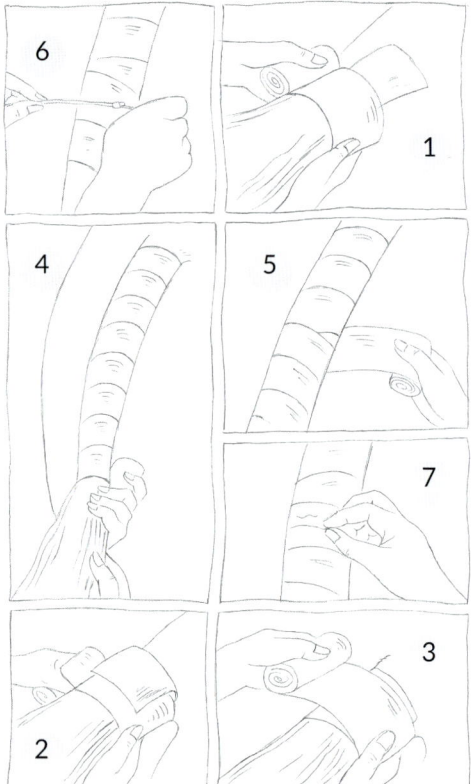

Q2.4

Untie. Bandage. Slide.

Q2.5

Fybagee for travelling can be shaped to fit over the knees and hocks, whereas Fybagee for stable bandages would not be shaped.

Q2.6

Too tight — restrict circulation; create pressure points or sores/rubs.
Too loose — not provide support, slip down or unravel.
Uneven tension — pressure points around leg creating sores or rubs.

Q2.7

POLL GUARD	— Prevents the horse from hurting his head if he should throw his head up and hit the ceiling of the horsebox/trailer.
LEATHER HEADCOLLAR	— Leather breaks in an emergency.
RUG	— Appropriate for time of year; maintains body temperature.
TAIL GUARD	— Gives extra protection to tail.
TAIL BANDAGE	— Protects the tail from rubbing.
TRAVEL BOOTS/BANDAGES	— Protect legs/hocks/knees/fetlocks/coronets from knocks.

Q2.8

Tie the horse up securely. On clean, dry legs fit each boot individually, positioning correctly and then fastening. When fastening, start with the middle strap and work up and down the leg from the centre out. Fasten firmly into position, ensuring no slippage.

Q2.9

The horse may tread on the boots and lose his footing.
The horse may need to alter his position and find that he cannot as he is treading on the opposite boot.
Poor quality boots may not stay up, leading to parts of the legs being unprotected.

Q2.10

RUGS	— Wash all rugs and reproof turnout rugs if required. Oil any leather straps.
BOOTS	— Synthetic: machine wash and air dry; leather: wash and saddle soap.
BANDAGES	— Machine wash and air dry.
FYBAGEE	— Machine wash and air dry.
ALL	— Should be stored in a cool, dry, vermin-proof area with moth balls. Leather oiled intermittently.

3 SADDLERY

Q3.1

SIZE	— Must be the right size for the horse.
LEVEL	— The saddle should sit level on the horse's back when viewed from the side and the back.
POMMEL CLEARANCE	— Two to three fingers between withers and pommel. One finger at each side of the withers.
GULLET	— Clear daylight through gullet.
SHOULDER	— Fits around shoulder.
BEARING SURFACE	— Even bearing surface from behind.

Q3.2

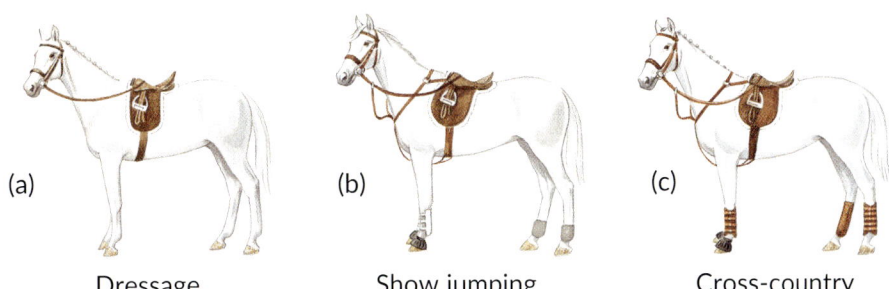

(a) Dressage (b) Show jumping (c) Cross-country

Q3.3

Horse is unhappy and does not perform well.
Horse's attitude changes — he becomes grumpy.
Horse bucks when ridden.
Sores develop, e.g. saddle, girth galls, and sores under the bridle.
Muscle wastage over the topline because the horse works incorrectly.

Q3.4

BRIDLE	— Fitted as normal, with a snaffle bit. Noseband removed. Reins tied up in the throatlash.
CAVESSON	— Noseband fitted two fingers' width below the projecting cheek bone. Buckles fastened under the cheek pieces and under the jaw, firmly.
SADDLE	— Fitted as normal, stirrups tied up.
SIDE REINS	— Attached under first girth strap and around the third. The clips should measure approximately a fists distance away from the bit when the horse is standing still. Clipped to the 'D' ring, across withers, when not in use.
BOOTS	— Brushing, fitted as normal.
LUNGE LINE	— Usually clipped onto centre ring of cavesson.

Q3.5

BIT	— Sit level in mouth, wrinkle in the corner of the lips, fit one finger either side.
BROWBAND	— Fit two fingers between forehead and brow band.
NOSEBAND	— Straight across face, fit two fingers between noseband and nose.
THROATLASH	— Fit four fingers between cheek and strap, runner and keeper fastened.
CHEEKPIECES	— Buckles level with eye, even on both sides, runners and keepers fastened.

Q3.6

FLASH	Sits slightly higher than normal cavesson, stop straps being pulled down, lower strap fastens in front of bit. Fit one finger between noseband and nose.
DROP	Fits approximately four fingers above top of the nostril, over the bony part of nose and not on the fleshy part. Fastens below bit under jaw. Fit two fingers between strap and nose.
GRACKLE	Top strap sits under the cheekpieces and fastens under cheek bones, lower straps fasten in chin groove. Rings should not interfere with projecting cheek bones. Fit one/two fingers between straps and horse's nose.

Q3.7

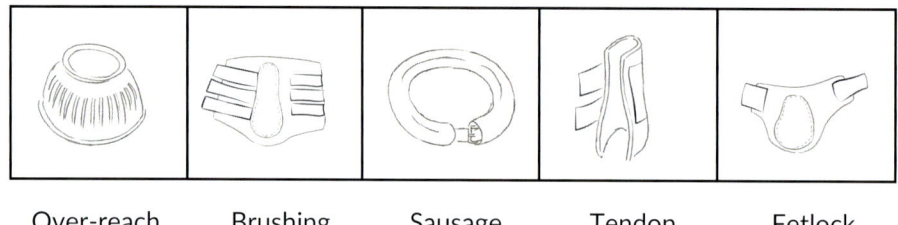

Over-reach   Brushing   Sausage   Tendon   Fetlock

OVER-REACH — Protect the heel from over-reaching injuries.
BRUSHING — Prevent damage when the horse brushes.
SAUSAGE — Put on one leg only, to help stop injuries to the coronet from the opposite foot.
TENDON — Used for show jumping. Protect the tendons down the back of the leg, whilst allowing the horse to feel if he knocks a pole with his cannons.
FETLOCK — For hind legs only; shortened boots that cover the fetlock only. Used solely for show jumping.

Q3.8

- Top of breastplate should sit just in front of the sensitive wither area.
- One hand's width between the neck strap and the horse.
- Girth loop should be approximately a hand's width from the chest.

Q3.9

WARM WATER — Cleans the tack, removes sweat and grime.
OIL — Supples and waterproofs.
SADDLE SOAP — Supples, waterproofs and shines.

Q3.10

Tack cleaned and heavily oiled.
Store under cover to prevent accumulation of dust, in a clean, dry area that will maintain a constant temperature.

4 HANDLING AND LUNGEING

Q4.1

RISK	MUCKING OUT	TACKING UP	LEADING
SELF	Horse could tread on you. Be aware. Always work in plenty of space or tie the horse outside the stable.	Horse could step on or bite you. Tie horse up. Work in plenty of space. Be aware.	External influence on the horse. Look for hazards. Anticipate.
HORSE	Tools. Use with care.	Horse could knock over saddle. Leave tack in safe place. Horse could react to girth being fastened. Fasten girth gently, have horse tied up. Horse could react to ill-fitting tack — check the fit regularly.	Hazards when leading. Change route. Remove hazards.
OTHERS	Tools used with care. Put away afterwards.	Horse reacts to incorrectly fitting tack when ridden. Make sure tack is put away on correct peg and check fit when tack up.	Horse reacts unexpectedly. Move horses at times when minimal number of people around.

Q4.2

Patient. Quiet. Relaxed. Efficient. Organised. Assertive.

Q4.3

Lower ramps carefully standing to the side.
Open partitions and secure.
Check loading area is safe and free from hazards.
Check horse area is safe.
String to tie horse up to.

Q4.4

Lead horse in a headcollar or bridle.
Stand next to horse's shoulder.
Lead up centre of the ramp.
Turn horse carefully into position (lorry).
Keep horse straight duck under breast bar (trailer).
Ask helper to secure partition/breech bar.
Tie horse up.

Q4.5

Carefully lower the ramp, stand to the side.
Untie horse.
Ask helper to undo partition or breast bar.
Stay by horse's shoulder.
Lead down centre of ramp.
Lead straight off bottom of ramp before turning.

Q4.6

To observe the horse working.
The horse has a sore back/saddle sores.
To improve suppleness.
To develop responsiveness to the voice.
When backing the horse.
To add variety in the work.
Rider unable to ride.
To take the edge off a fresh horse.
Build up muscle.

Q4.7

A	B
Standing tall	Slouching
Eye contact	Eyes to the ground
Hands in correct position	Hands too high
Shoulders back, looking assertive	Round shoulders, meek
Whip in position to be effective	Whip ineffective
Standing square to the horse	Standing side on

Q4.8

Consistent. Accepting.

Q4.9

The horse must stay at the end of the lunge line.
The horse must respond correctly to commands.

Q4.10

WALK	— Warm up and cool down. The horse must get used to walking on the lunge.
TROT	— Exercise, suppleness, balance and rhythm. The main pace used when lungeing.
CIRCLE	— Suppleness, rhythm, balance, engagement.
TRANSITIONS	— Responsiveness to the aids, engagement.
CANTER	— Can be used to encourage more energy in the trot in a lazy horse, or to take the edge off a fresh horse.

Q4.11

CAVESSON	— Leaves the bit free for the side reins. No pressure on the mouth.
SIDE REINS	— Provide the horse with a contact to work into and therefore produce an outline and develop a correct way of going. Acceptance of the contact.
BRUSHING BOOTS	— Protection.
LUNGE LINE	— Dictates the shape and size of the circle.
SADDLE/ROLLER	— Introduction to tack. Point of attachment for the side reins. Saddle required if lungeing a rider.
LUNGE WHIP	— Reinforces the lunger's voice.

Q4.12

Protection.

5 STABLE DESIGN

Q5.1

	ADVANTAGES	DISADVANTAGES
WALLS		
Breeze Block	Relatively inexpensive.	Porous, therefore not suitable for external walls.
Brick	Excellent temperature regulation; durable	Expensive.
Wood	Cheap, quick to erect.	Not fire resistant; poor temperature regulation; encourages wood chewing.
ROOF		
Tiles	Good temperature regulation.	Potential hazard in high winds.
Plywood and Felt	Relatively inexpensive.	Fire hazard.
Onduline	Light weight, flexible, can have clear plastic inserts to provide natural light.	Can cause condensation if not lined.
FLOOR		
Brick	Durable; fireproof; good temperature regulation.	Expensive; not ideal for horses to stand on for long periods.
Concrete	Durable; less expensive than bricks.	Not ideal for horses to stand on for long periods.
Rubber Matting	Add layer of protection between floor and horse, make floor a bit warmer, long lasting.	Urine and bedding can collect underneath unless mats are lifted and cleaned under regularly. Mats can stretch and warp over time.

Q5.2

	16 hh HORSE	PONY
SIZE	12ft x 12ft (3.6 x 3.6m)	10ft x 12ft (3m x 3.6m)
HEIGHT	15ft (4.5m)	12ft (3.6m)
DOOR WIDTH	4ft (1.2m)	4ft (1.2m)
DOOR HEIGHT	10ft (3m)	8ft (2.4m)
HALF DOOR HEIGHT	4ft 6ins (1.37m)	3ft-3ft 6ins (0.9m-1.06m)

ANSWERS / 6 SHOEING

Q5.3

(a)
Half door.
Slatted window and bars.
Ventilated corrugated sheeting.
Roof vents.
Louvre boards.

(b)
The horse should not breathe stale air.
Prevents the spread of disease and aids recuperation.

Q5.4

(a)
To remove waste water. Slopes backward so urine is removed and horse does not stand in it when looking over the door.

(b)
Stagnant waste water.
Ill-health and disease.
Damp environment.
Respiratory disorders.
Feed/hay becomes damp and turns sour.
Use more bedding.

Q5.5

ESSENTIAL	EXTRA
Tie ring with string	Extra tie ring for haynet
Watering system — buckets/automatic waterer	Feed manger
	Hay rack

Q5.6

Less to potentially harm the horse.

6 SHOEING

Q6.1

 BUFFER

 DRIVING HAMMER / PINCERS

 DRAWING KNIFE / RASP / NAIL CLENCHER

A   BUFFER — Raises clenches.
B   DRIVING HAMMER — Used with buffer to raise clenches. Hammers nails into hoof. Trims the ends of nails.
C   PINCERS — Levers off the shoe.
D   DRAWING KNIFE — Trims the horn, sole and frog.
E   RASP — Levels the surface of the foot and finishes off around the edge once the shoe is on.
F   NAIL CLENCHER — Folds the nail ends over so the clench is flush with the hoof wall.

Q6.2

Place foot between knees if front foot, rest on thigh if back foot.
Raise all clenches using the buffer and hammer.
Use the pincers to remove the shoe, levering both heels a quarter of the way down the shoe, inwards.

Q6.3

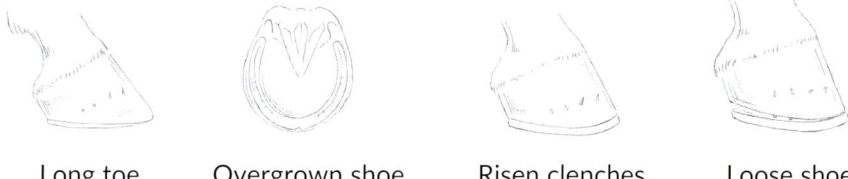

Long toe   Overgrown shoe   Risen clenches   Loose shoe

Q6.4

LONG TOE	— Pressure on the tendons and ligaments at the back of the leg and on the hoof wall. Broken hoof/pastern axis.
OVERGROWN SHOE	— The shoe sits inside the wall, on the sole, causing bruising.
RISEN CLENCHES	— The shoe becomes loose and the movement can cause bruising.
LOOSE SHOE	— Shoes come off, often breaking away some of the hoof. Can be dangerous to ride, as the horse will lose purchase on the ground.

Q6.5

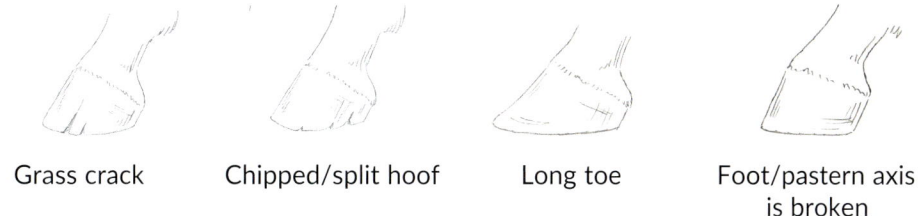

Grass crack   Chipped/split hoof   Long toe   Foot/pastern axis is broken

7 TRIMMING

Q7.1

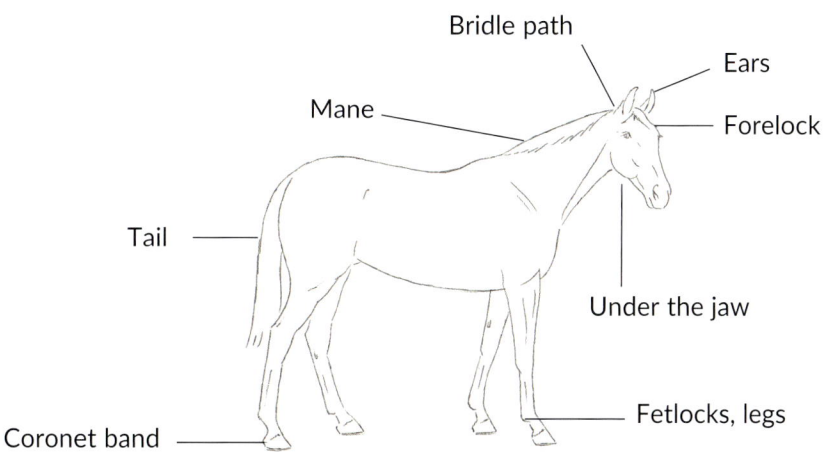

ANSWERS/8 ANATOMY AND PHYSIOLOGY

Q7.2

Ears	— Gently press outer edges together and trim long hairs off.
Jaw	— Use clippers or scissors to trim long hair.
Bridle path	— Using scissors or small trimmers cut small patch behind the poll.
Legs	— Comb hair upwards and trim with scissors or clip against direction of hair.
Tail	— Use scissors or clippers to trim ends.
Mane	— Use comb and scissors to trim or mane comb to pull or comb with blade.

Q7.3

Some native breeds. (Native breeds are not shown trimmed.)
In winter a horse who lives out. The hair provides protection and warmth

Q7.4

CORRECT	INCORRECT
Shows off the horse's neck.	Makes the mane longer.
Thins the mane.	Makes the mane thicker.
Makes the mane lie better.	Makes the mane less greasy.
Easier to plait.	

8 ANATOMY AND PHYSIOLOGY

Q8.1

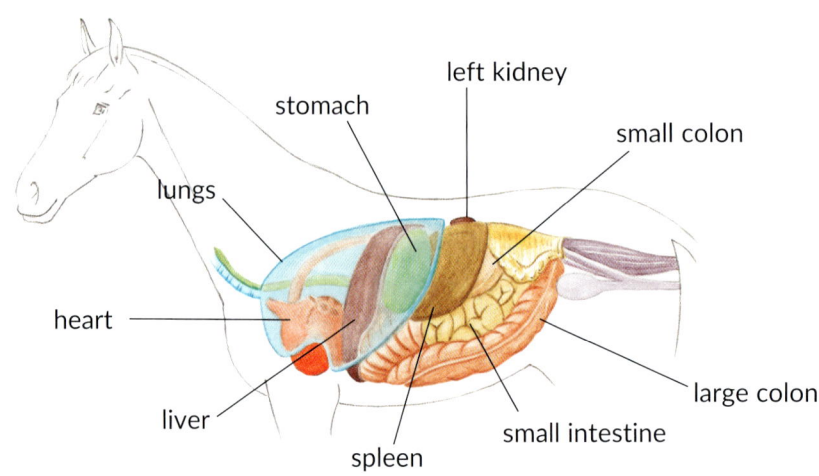

Q8.2

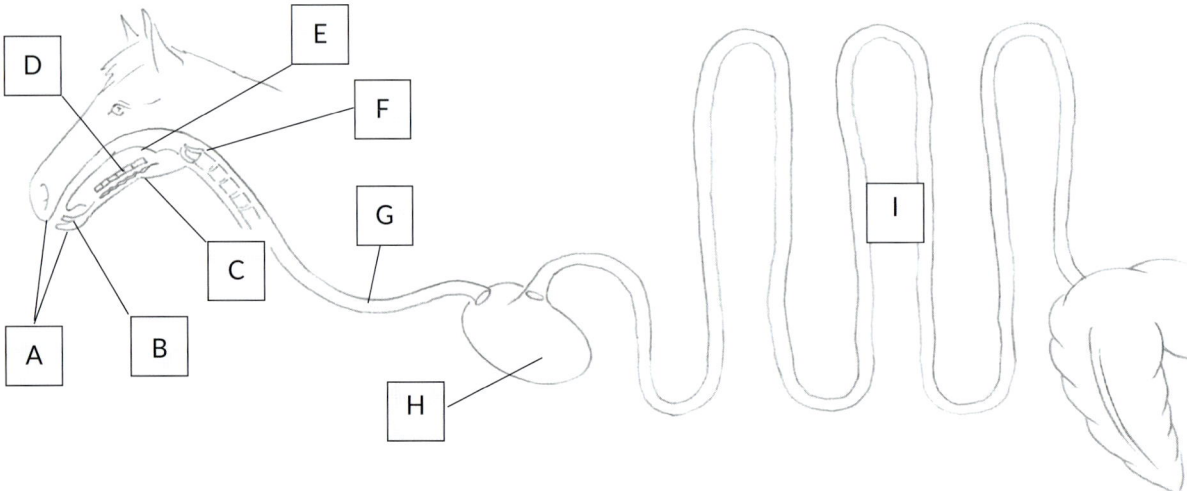

ANSWERS/8 ANATOMY AND PHYSIOLOGY

A LIPS — Gather food.
B INCISORS — Crop grass.
C SALIVARY GLANDS — Lubricates food.
D MOLARS — Grind.
E TONGUE — Passes bolus of food to the back of the mouth.
F EPIGLOTTIS — Covers trachea as food passes over and into the oesophagus.
G OESOPHAGUS — Via peristalsis (waves of muscular contractions along the oesophagus), passes food from the mouth to the stomach.
H STOMACH — Gastric juices begin the breakdown of food.
I SMALL INTESTINE — Further food breakdown by enzyme secretions; absorbs carbohydrates, proteins and fats.

Q8.3

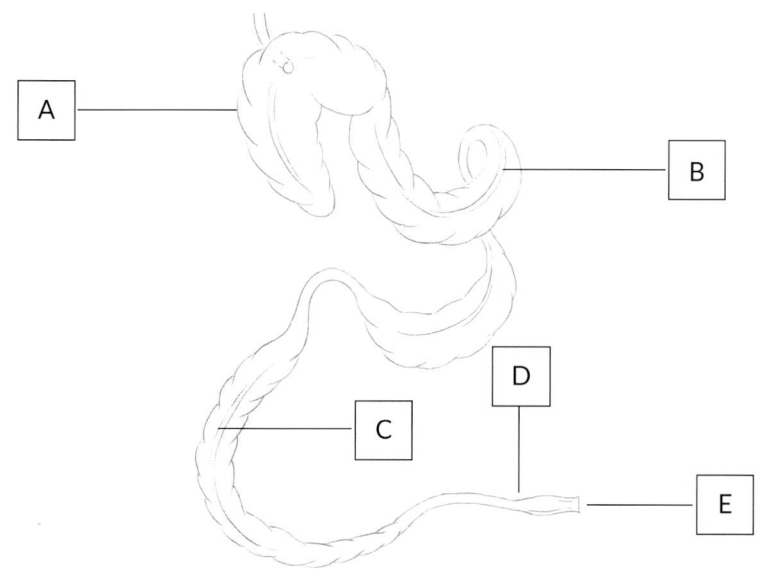

A CAECUM — Bacteria break down cellulose in grass, hay and haylage — hence need to change diet slowly as bacteria need to change. Nutrients and water absorbed.
B LARGE COLON — Further bacterial breakdown, nutrients and water absorbed. Pelvic flexure is a narrowing in the colon and possible area of blockage.
C SMALL COLON — Absorbs electrolytes and water.
D RECTUM — Waste matter stored before expulsion.
E ANUS — Sphincter muscle regulates waste expulsion.

Q8.4

The horse's digestive system has evolved to function best on a diet of forage/fibre. The digestive system is designed to have fibre moving slowly through it continually to allow food to be broken down and absorbed efficiently.

ANSWERS/8 ANATOMY AND PHYSIOLOGY

Q8.5

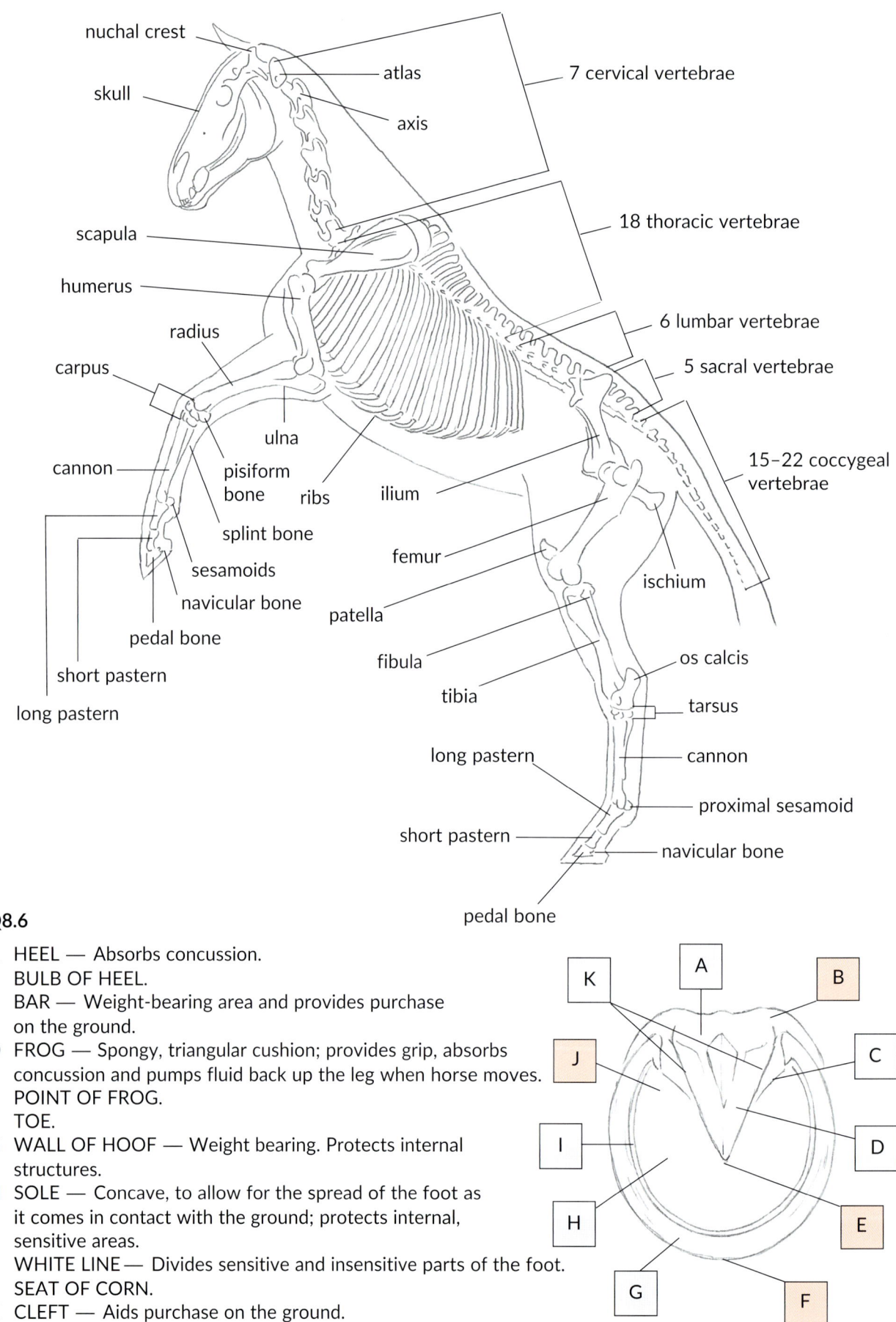

Q8.6

A HEEL — Absorbs concussion.
B BULB OF HEEL.
C BAR — Weight-bearing area and provides purchase on the ground.
D FROG — Spongy, triangular cushion; provides grip, absorbs concussion and pumps fluid back up the leg when horse moves.
E POINT OF FROG.
F TOE.
G WALL OF HOOF — Weight bearing. Protects internal structures.
H SOLE — Concave, to allow for the spread of the foot as it comes in contact with the ground; protects internal, sensitive areas.
I WHITE LINE — Divides sensitive and insensitive parts of the foot.
J SEAT OF CORN.
K CLEFT — Aids purchase on the ground.

9 HORSE BEHAVIOUR

Q9.1

Flies.
Heat.
Bickering.

Q9.2

	NATURAL LIFESTYLE	STABLE
Exercise programme	Nomadic	Structured exercise
Feed/water	Nomadic/grazers	Eats when fed
Breeding	Natural selection	Breeding programmes
Grooming	Groom each other	Grooming from staff, including trimming as required
Contact	Within herd	Only with companions during turnout
Feet	Natural wear	Artificial shoeing
Predators/disease	Predators in the wild/survival of the fittest	No predators/veterinary treatments
Instincts	Follow natural instincts	Overcome natural instincts through training, e.g. clipping, wearing rugs

Q9.3

STABLE	— Rolls eyes. Head high. Body tense. Turns quarters in fear, ready to fight because he cannot flee.
FIELD	— Runs to the furthest end of the field away from danger, then turns and looks.
RIDDEN IN THE SCHOOL	— Head up, tries to flee.
RIDDEN ON THE ROAD	— Spooks. Bolts.
JUMPING	— Refuses, runs out, jumps higher than necessary.
BEING LED	— Head up, tries to flee, spooks.

Q9.4

Excited and enjoying being in the field. Likes companionship. Does not want to return to the stable.
Frightened of the person catching him.

Q9.5

(a) Horse grasps an object with its teeth and pulls back, gulps air and makes a grunting noise.
(b) Horse walks repeatedly around its stable in a circle.
(c) Horse stands and moves weight from one front leg to the other, swinging head and neck at same time.

Q9.6

Not socialised with other horses.
Not socialised in a ridden environment.
Intimidated by other horses coming too close.
Views the ride as a herd and tries to establish a pecking order.
Uncomfortable with tack/rider and is therefore grumpy.

Q9.7

Nips as the girth is done up from the ground.
Bucks.
Rears.
Bolts.
Open mouth.

Humps over back.
Takes short strides.
Not wishing to go forwards.
Reluctant to respond to aids.

10 HORSE HEALTH

Q10.1

Exercise correctly.
Follow the rules of feeding.
Follow a worming programme.
Routine checks — dentist, chiropractor.
Regular attention to the horse's feet.
Rug appropriately.
Clip appropriately.

Q10.2

TEMPERATURE	37.5–38.5°C (99.5–100.5°F)	Time of day, raised when worked, raised if fever, higher in foals.
PULSE	28–44 BPM	Time of day, raised when worked, raised if ill, anxious, higher in foals, lower if very fit.
RESPIRATION	8–16 BPM	Time of day, raised when worked, raised if ill, anxious, higher in foals, lower if very fit.

Q10.3

BREATHING	Increase due to pain/respiratory problems.
EATING	An unwell horse does not want to eat normally.
DRINKING	Increase/decrease in amount drunk could indicate ill-health.
DROPPINGS	More/less than normal or change in consistency suggests a change in diet or digestive system.
STANCE	Resting a hind leg is normal, but not the same one all the time. Resting a foreleg ('pointing a foot') indicates a problem. Head down and dull or 'tucked up' indicates ill-health.

Q10.4

Horse repeatedly lying down and getting up.
Rolling.
Kicking at the belly.
Looking round at flanks.
Pawing the ground.
Walking around the stable.
Sweating.
Not eating or drinking.
Increase in breathing.
Not passing any droppings.
Dull or depressed.

Q10.5

Follow the rules of feeding.
Ensure routine health procedures such as worming and dental checks are carried out.
Make changes to turnout routines gradually.
Ensure the horse is exercised regularly and cooled off properly before feeding.

Q10.6

PUNCTURE WOUND	Caused by sharp object e.g. nail/thorn. Look small on surface but can be very deep. Serious if occur to joint.
OPEN WOUND	Cut or tear. Bleed heavily. May need to be stitched.
GRAZE	Superficial wound involving the top layers of skin. Usually contain debris and require cleaning thoroughly.
BRUISE	Caused by trauma e.g. kick. Underlying tissues and blood vessels damaged causing pain and swelling.

Q10.7

CLEANING A CUT	If needs stitching call a vet, clean from inside out, using gauze (non fluffy), using a fresh piece each time, use clean, fresh water, apply sterile dressing if required. Can cold hose to clean depending on location.
COLD HOSING	Start small trickle down by hoof, gradually move up above the area, increase flow gradually to steady flow. 5–10 minutes.
TUBBING	Use shallow skip, place horses foot in, fill with warm water (up to coronary band), add enough Epsom salts to form a sludge, (follow supervisor advice). 5 minutes.
POULTICING	Cut poultice to slightly larger than size of area to be covered, place in cooled boiled water, squeeze out excess water. Place poultice over area (make sure area is clean) shiny side facing out and secure. Should not be used over a joint as risk of drawing out joint fluid.

Q10.8

(a) Nothing, unless you need to stop bleeding or it could become further infected without a dressing, in which case, use a sterile, dry dressing and apply pressure as necessary. Do not use creams or coloured sprays otherwise the vet cannot see the wound clearly.
(b) Tetanus.

Q10.9

Convalescence diet: 100% fibre immediately. Roughage — meadow hay — easy to chew and palatable.
Constant supply of fresh, clean water.
Clean, hygienic environment.
Ventilation without draughts.
Keep the horse warm — layer light rugs.

Dust-free hay and bedding.
Follow veterinary instructions.
Do not pester. Only one person to attend to the horse if possible.
Isolate horse if required.
Keep records of any medication given.
Monitor and record temperature, pulse and respiration (TPR).

Q10.10

First signs of colic	— Vet.
Minor lameness	— Monitor.
Horse seen quidding	— Teeth checked by a vet or equine dental technician.
Severe lameness	— Vet.
Minor graze to the quarters	— Basic treatment.
Suspected broken leg	— Vet.
Horse a little dull	— Monitor.
Serious arterial bleed	— Vet.

Q10.11

Medical history — veterinary treatments, ill-health and its duration.
Shoeing.
Vaccinations.
Dental treatment.
Chiropractic treatment.
Horse's normal TPR.
Horse's normal weight.
Saddle checks.

Q10.12

Alter wormer to correct amount, headcollar on horse, place arm around horses nose, place wormer in corner of mouth facing towards back of mouth, dispense plunger, lift horses head up to encourage swallowing.

Q10.13

Worm egg counts.
Following worming programme.
Regular dropping removal from fields.
Rotate/rest grazing paddocks.
Cross grazing with sheep or cattle.

Q10.14

Not accepting the contact when ridden; fussy in the mouth when ridden.
Quidding — the horse drops half-chewed food out of his mouth.
Takes a longer time to eat than normal.
Loss of appetite.
Bad smell from mouth.
Food stacked up in pouches in the sides of the mouth, like a hamster.

Q10.15

As the horse grinds his food, the outer edges of the upper jaw teeth and the inner edges of the lower jaw teeth are not worn down like the rest of the surface of the tooth because the upper jaw is slightly larger than the lower jaw. The equine dental technician/vet rasps to make the teeth even.

11 FITTENING

Q11.1

Reduced co-ordination.
Slowing down.
Increased breathing effort.
Brushing or over reaching.
Unwilling to perform e.g. jump.
Increased head and neck movement.

Q11.2

HACKING	Work over variety of terrain, less stressful than in a school, improve balance and co-ordination, build muscle and stamina.
SCHOOLING	Build muscle, improve way of going.
JUMP/POLE WORK	Improve co-ordination, build strength, improve suppleness, variety.
LUNGEING	Variety, allows horse to work without weight of rider, work horses in fairly short time.

Q11.3

If the horse is overweight or underweight.
Current fitness level.
Previous injury.
Existing health condition.

Q11.4

Change of environment from field to stable.
Change of feed — grass to hay.
Physical pressure — lungs working harder.
Stress.

Q11.5

Skin softened during time off.
Horse has changed shape and tack may not fit perfectly.
Tack may need attention if not well cared for.

Q11.6

CONCUSSION
Road work in trot.
Hard ground.
Jumping on a hard surface.
Fast work on hard ground.

STRAIN/SPRAIN
Deep going.
Jumping on a soft surface.
Fast work in deep going.
Trotting downhill.

Q11.7

Horse should be walked until breathing returns to normal — not blowing. This could be ridden, in hand or on a horse walker depending on circumstances and facilities.

ANSWERS / 12 GRASSLAND CARE

Q11.8

Remove tack and clean later.
Wash as necessary — not cold water.
Return to stable, rug as necessary and leave to relax.
Groom and check the horse over. Look for areas of heat or swelling, particularly the legs.

12 GRASSLAND CARE

Q12.1

- Variety of quality grasses.
- Good grass density all over.
- All lawns, no roughs.
- No droppings — good picking up policy lessens the chance of worms and keeps grass sweet.
- Gently sloping land for free drainage.
- Good location for an automatic water trough.
- Well maintained post and rail fencing with electric fencing on the top to prevent chewing or leaning over the fence.
- Natural shelter from hedges on three sides, offering protection from sun, wind, rain.
- Free from poisonous plants.
- Gateway access 5-bar gate with padlocks both sides.

Q12.2

Cutting hedges encourages greater density. Hedges need to be kept back from fencing, especially electric, otherwise they can short the current, making it ineffective.

Q12.3

- Land, for poaching.
- Grass — Length and density — is there enough to sustain the horses, or does the land need a rest?
- Water trough — Functioning?
- Fencing — Intact?
- Field shelter — Safe?
- No poisonous plants.
- Horses — Right number and all healthy.
- Droppings — Daily or weekly removal.
- Litter and rubbish — Daily removal.

Q12.4

Ragwort   Deadly Nightshade   Bracken   Foxglove

Q12.5

GOOD   BAD

Perennial ryegrass   Timothy   Meadow fescue   Cocksfoot   Bent   Yorkshire fog

13 FEEDING

Q13.1

SUGAR BEET	By product of the sugar refining process. Must be soaked before feeding. Comes in shreds, flakes or pellets.
ALFALFA	Chopped up Lucerne grass. Fed dried and chopped to bulk out feed and encourage horse to chew or fed as pellets. Good source of protein.
CHAFF	Chopped up hay and straw. Can have molasses mixed in. Good to bulk out feed and encourage horse to chew.
GRASS NUTS	Cut grass formed into pellets. Tend to be slightly green in colour. Useful for horses who can't eat long stem fibre e.g. older horses.

Q13.2

CEREAL	DESCRIPTION
Barley	Flat, round flakes, golden in colour. Needs to be treated before feeding. Can be fed on its own as a straight.
Oats	Long, thin golden golden in colour. Can be fed as it is or treated. Can be fed on its own as a straight.
Maize	Bright yellow flakes, usually found in a mix or cubes. Very high in energy.
Peas/Beans	Green flakes found in mix or cubes. Provide protein.

Q13.3

(a)
Digestive system less efficient.
Teeth may be less able to grind properly.
Generally lose weight as they get older.
May need higher level of protein.

(b)
Meadow hay — softer to chew.
Haylage — high nutritional value.
Wet feed — sugar beet.
Alfalfa — high in protein — older horses may need higher levels of protein.
Veteran mix — especially formulated for older horses.

Q13.4

Reduce amount of bucket feed given. Feed forage ad lib.

Q13.5

Weigh tape.
Weigh bridge.
Formula: weight (kg) = (girth (cm))^2 x length (cm)/11877.

ANSWERS/13 FEEDING

Q13.6

Horse	Bodyweight (Kg)	1% of bodyweight (bodyweight ÷ 100 x 1)	(2% of bodyweight) Minimum amount of forage to feed (Kg)
BRODY	650	6.5	13
CANDY	320	3.2	6.4
FLYNN	280	2.8	5.6
SUNNY	500	5	10
EBONY	540	5.4	10.8

Q13.7

	HAY	HAYLAGE	SILAGE
SUITABLE FOR HORSES	Yes	Yes	No, but some feed if horses used to it; can be problematic
MOISTURE (%)	15	60	80

Q13.8

	GALLEON		LUCA		SIGI		DEXTER		MELODY	
	am + lunch	pm	am + lunch	pm	am + lunch	pm	am + lunch	pm	am	pm
HAYLAGE lbs (kg)	5 (2.2)	10 (4.5)	5 (2.2)	10 (4.5)	5 (2.2)	10 (4.5)	5 (2.2)	8 (3.6)	4 (1.8)	8 (3.6)
PONY NUTS lbs (kg)	3 (1.3)	4 (1.8)	3 (1.3)	4 (1.8)	3 (1.3)	4 (1.8)				
COMPETITION MIX – lbs (kg)							3 (1.3)	3 (1.3)		
ALFALFA lbs (kg)							1 (0.45)	1 (0.45)		
SUPPLEMENTS							10g electrolyte			
CARROTS									2	2

14 RIDING

Q14.1

Giving signals when riding on the road.
Riding and leading.

Q14.2

A whip is an object to inflict pain on the horse. FALSE
A whip is used only to make a horse go faster. FALSE
The whip should be used behind the leg to reinforce the leg aid. TRUE
The use of the whip should not interfere with the contact on the reins. TRUE

Q14.3

Consistency.
Repetition.
Positive reinforcement.
Patience.
Routine.
Honesty.

Q14.4

Pass left to left.
The outer track is for the faster paces.
Turn across the school for downward transitions.
The inner track is for the slower paces.
The outer track has right of way.
Lateral work has right of way.

Q14.5

Use outer area of the field for the faster paces — that is, do not canter across the field.
To prevent accidents do not canter closely past another horse.
Use school figures to change the rein to maintain balance.

Q14.6

Downhill	Faster, less balanced.
Uphill	Slower, balanced.
Slippery, greasy	Unbalanced.
Heavy, deep	Slower, unbalanced.
Hard	Slower or faster, balanced.

Q14.7

NAME	DESCRIPTION
Rhythm	The regularity of the gait.
Suppleness	The horse's ability to bend evenly on each side.
Contact	The feel you have down the rein.
Impulsion	The energy within a gait.
Straightness	The horse's hind legs follow the tracks of the front feet.
Collection	The horse lowers his hind quarters and takes more weight behind.

Q14.8

Inside leg	— Used next to the girth, asks the horse to move forward and to bend.
Outside leg	— Used slightly behind the girth, controls the quarters.
Outside rein	— Controls outside shoulder and speed of the horse.
Inside rein	— Asks for flexion, guides the direction of the horse.

Q14.9

1. The horse falling in/falling out.
2. Circle incorrect size/shape.
3. Circle not symmetrical.
4. Horse drifting through the shoulder.

Q14.10

The canter should be forward, balanced and rhythmical. During the turn on the approach to the fence, the quality of the canter is maintained by keeping the horse balanced between leg and hand. On the straight line approach, again the quality of the canter is maintained. The rider guides the horse to the centre of the fence and should look up and over the jump, focusing on the departure. As the horse jumps, the rider moves forward into jumping position, allowing the horse's head to move forward whilst maintaining a light contact at the end of the reins. The rider helps the horse to jump by remaining in balance with the horse. Maintaining a secure lower leg position allows the rider to land in balance and immediately rebalance the horse between leg and hand, recognise the canter lead and change it if necessary, using the next corner. The canter rhythm is re-established, if necessary, and a straight line ridden away from the fence, maintaining the quality of the canter through the departure turn.

Q14.11

To allow the rider to adopt and maintain a balanced jumping position.

Q14.12

Approach	Horse should be straight and active. Rider aiming for the centre of fence.
Take off	The horse pushes off with hind legs and lifts forehand and folds front legs. Rider starts to fold.
Flight	Horse makes a bascule shape over fence, stretches head and neck forward for balance. Rider should fold to stay in balance and allow hands forward.
Landing	Front legs land and horse lifts head and neck. Rider starts to sit up.
Getaway	Horse moves away from the fence in straight line. Rider looking towards next fence and rides horse actively forward.

Q14.13

Refusal.
Run out.
Poor jump.
Rider unbalanced over the fence.

Q14.14

RIDER:
Secure and balanced position.
Ability to use lower leg effectively.
Maintaining a consistent contact throughout.
Confidence.

HORSE:
Balanced
Forward.
Rhythmical.
Good quality canter.
Desire to jump.

FURTHER READING

The following books can all be obtained from the BHS Bookshop (address overleaf).

  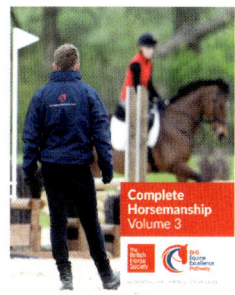 

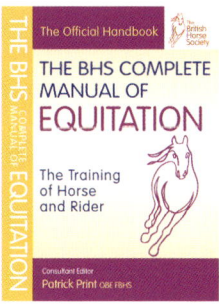  

USEFUL ADDRESSES

The British Horse Society
Equestrian House
Abbey Park
Stareton
Kenilworth
Warwickshire
CV8 2XZ
tel: 02476 840500
website: www.bhs.org.uk
email: enquiry@bhs.org.uk

BHS Equine Excellence Team
(address as above)
tel: 02476 840508
email: pathways@bhs.org.uk

BHS Approvals Department
(address as above)
tel: 02476 840509
email: approvals@bhs.org.uk

BHS Bookshop
(address as above)
tel: 02476 840513
website: www.britishhorse.com

NOTES

NOTES